We'll Race You, HENRY

We'll Race You, HENRY

A Story about Henry Ford

by Barbara Mitchell

illustrations by Kathy Haubrich

A Carolrhoda Creative Minds Book

Carolrhoda Books, Inc./Minneapolis

For Dr. DeSanctis and his Model A

Text copyright © 1986 by Barbara Mitchell
Illustrations copyright © 1986 by Carolrhoda Books, Inc.
Manufactured in the United States of America

This book is available in two editions:
Library binding by Carolrhoda Books, Inc.
Soft cover by First Avenue Editions
241 First Avenue North
Minneapolis, Minnesota 55401

LIBRARY OF CONGRESS CATALOGING-IN-PUBLICATION DATA

Mitchell, Barbara, 1941-
    We'll race you, Henry.

    (A Carolrhoda creative minds book)
    Summary: A brief biography of Henry Ford with emphasis
on how he came to develop fast, sturdy, and reliable
racing cars that eventually gave him the idea for his
Model T.
    1. Ford, Henry, 1863-1947—Biography—Juvenile
literature. 2. Automobile industry and trade—United
States—Biography—Juvenile literature. [1. Ford,
Henry, 1863-1947. 2. Automobile industry and trade—
Biography] I. Haubrich, Kathy, ill. II. Title.
III. Series.
TL140.F6M58   1986   338.7'6292'0924 [B] [92]   86-2691
ISBN 0-87614-291-9 (lib. bdg.)
ISBN 0-87614-471-7 (pbk.)

        4   5   6   7   8   9   10   96   95   94   93   92   91   90

Table of Contents

Chapter One

It was long past bedtime on the Ford farm. The Homestead was dark, except for the oil lamp that glowed in eleven-year-old Henry's room. Henry was up experimenting again at his secret window workshop.

His mother's voice came down the hall. "Henry—you still up?"

Henry quickly folded the collapsible legs of the worktable cluttered with disassembled windup toys and shoved the whole thing under his bed. He blew out the oil lamp and the lantern that kept his feet warm and climbed in under the quilts. Farm boys were supposed to be in bed early. Farm work began before sunup.

Henry did not care for farm work. He thought it was boring. Every morning and every evening he squatted on a milk stool. He leaned into the side of one cow, then another, and another. "Cow," Henry would say, "someday somebody will invent a better way to get milk."

Henry hated plowing, too. He spent long days plodding up one row and down another, looking at the back end of a horse. "Horse," Henry would say, "someday I will invent something that will make farm life more fun."

Henry loved mechanical things: springs and gears and cogs and wheels, things that clicked and ticked and turned. The Fords had a farmhand who liked to bring the children treats. "What can I bring you from Detroit?" their friend would ask.

"Peppermints!" cried Henry's little sisters.

"Licorice whips!" cried Henry's little brothers.

"Clock wheels," said Henry.

Back would come a bag of clock wheels for Henry. It wasn't long before Henry knew all about what made clocks tick and how to fix them when they didn't.

Every time Henry could manage it, he went to Detroit himself. Sometimes he skated down the frozen River Rouge and onto the Detroit River. Sometimes he walked the whole eight miles to visit the steamy trainyards, shipyards, and boiler factories. Huffing-puffing, clanging-banging Detroit. Henry loved every bit of it. "Someday I will go there to live," he said.

One hot summer day in 1876, Henry and his father were riding to Detroit in the farm wagon. Suddenly there was a huffing-puffing monster heading straight toward them. It was a steam engine. Henry knew that. Steam engines were used on the farm to help with the harvesting. But those engines were hauled to the fields by horses. This one was a road-roller, and it was lumbering down the road all by itself. There wasn't *anything* pulling it!

Thirteen-year-old Henry was down off that wagon before his father even knew what he was up to. A machine that could go down the road all by itself was something to find out about. That was the day Henry started thinking about horseless riding machines—and he never stopped.

Chapter Two

When he was sixteen, Henry went to Detroit to live. There he got a job with a company that made streetcars. Soon Henry knew all about making streetcars. "Now I've got to learn about how things are made from metal," Henry said. So he left the streetcar company and got a job at a foundry that made everything from fire hydrants to boat whistles out of brass and iron. Next Henry went to the Detroit Dry Dock Engine Works. The Dry Dock Works was just crammed full of all kinds of machines. Henry not only did his own work, but found time to watch other workers using their skills as well. By the summer of 1882, Henry felt he had learned all he could possibly learn about machines.

Back on the farm, Henry's father worried about him. It was time Henry settled down to the business of being a farmer. What kind of farmer hung around machine shops, anyway?

"I'll give you 40 acres of good land if you'll just come home and forget about this machine business," he told Henry.

Henry went back to the farm. He even cleared his land. But young Henry's farm was a strange one. There were no cows for milking. There were no horses for plowing. There was not even a rooster to crow at the sun. What Henry's farm did have was a machine shop. "It's first rate," he told his father proudly.

Mr. Ford shook his head. "That Henry," he said. "I don't know what's to become of him."

The neighbors wondered about Henry, too. "That Ford boy has wheels in the head," they said.

Even Henry's friends complained about him. "It's no fun going to sociables with Henry," they said. "All he talks about is his gas buggy."

Henry had begun experimenting with little gasoline engines. He had the idea they could be used to pull a horseless buggy. The gas buggy idea may have hampered his conversation, but it did nothing to spoil his dancing. Henry was an expert dancer. On New Year's night in 1885, Henry went to a party. There he met another good dancer, a young woman named Clara Jane Bryant.

Not only could Clara keep up with Henry's fancy dance steps, she loved hearing all about his gas buggy as well.

In the spring of 1888, Henry and Clara were married. They settled down on Henry's farm. Henry spent his days repairing steam engines for other farmers. At night he read books on mechanics. Both Henry and Clara loved music, and Clara often sat playing the organ while Henry read his scientific magazines. "Clara!" Henry said one evening, "I think I know how to make the engine to run my gas buggy." He took a sheet of Clara's music and sketched a little engine. "We *will* need to move in to Detroit, though," Henry added. "I've got to learn all about electricity."

There was no electricity out in the country in 1889. In fact, Detroit was only just becoming illuminated. Electricity as a power source was still experimental. Henry knew that Thomas Edison, the "electrical wizard," was conducting electrical experiments at his Detroit company. (Edison was not to invent the light bulb until 1893.) Henry was hoping to use electricity to spark the power for his gasoline engine.

Clara was happy being a farmwife, but she believed with all her heart in Henry's ideas. "Very well, Henry," she said, and she began packing for the move to the city.

Henry got a job at the Detroit Illuminating Company. He would be working under Edison himself! Henry kept a personal workshop on the job, where he could experiment in his free time, and one in the woodshed at home, too. He spent every free moment working on his gas engine.

One chilly fall night in 1893, a doctor made a visit to the Ford house. By dawn, Henry and Clara had a baby boy. They named him Edsel after Henry's closest boyhood friend. Henry watched the tired doctor climb back onto his bike and ride off to another patient. "Someday I will find a better way for doctors to get about in the middle of the night," he said.

On Christmas Eve, Henry was in his woodshed working as usual. Clara was bustling about in the kitchen. Their relatives were coming for Christmas dinner. There was the turkey to stuff, the cranberries to jell, and the pies to make. Baby Edsel lay sleeping nearby.

In came Henry, all greasy and grimy, his gas engine in hand. He clamped the engine to Clara's clean kitchen sink. "I need you to dribble gasoline into the engine," he explained.

Clara didn't say a word. She just took hold of the oilcan Henry handed her.

"Now, turn the screw like this," Henry instructed. He connected a wire to the kitchen light. VROOM! The light blinked. The sink shook. Baby Edsel let out a wail. It worked! Henry picked up his precious engine and carried it back to the shop.

He got busy making a body for the gas buggy. Henry had to figure out how to make the wheels, the seat, the steering—everything—from scratch. His workshop light was often on all night long now. "Don't wait supper," he would tell Clara. "I'll just get a bite at Night Owl John's Diner."

Little by little, the gas buggy began to take shape. Henry moved the project into his garage now. At four o'clock one morning in the spring of 1896, Henry, Clara, and a friend named Jim Bishop gathered around the gas buggy. It was finished. Henry vaulted over the side and slid into the driver's seat. (Henry always vaulted his way into cars, even when he was 80 years old.) He had been working for nearly three years for this moment. "Roll 'er out," he said to Jim Bishop. Then Henry and Jim looked at the door ahead of them. It was much too small for the gas buggy to go through!

Henry jumped down from the gas buggy. He grabbed an axe and chopped a hole in the wall right beside that door! He vaulted back into the buggy. Jim gave a push, and the gas buggy rolled out into the cobblestone alley. Henry gave his horseless riding machine the gas and went chugging out onto the rain-splashed streets of Detroit.

Chapter Three

Every time Henry and his horseless buggy appeared, they caused a sensation. Ladies hurried to the sidewalk. Horses reared. The Detroit policemen kept a wary eye. "You're not to drive that thing faster than five miles an hour," they warned Henry. The gas buggy had no brakes. To stop it, Henry simply cut off the gas. Then he jumped over the side and tied the buggy to a pole the way he would a horse. If he didn't tie it, it was likely to roll away.

Henry wasn't the only one experimenting with horseless riding machines. Mechanics all over the country, and in Europe, too, were tinkering with ways to hitch their buggies up to steam engines, electric engines, and gas engines. The problem was that these new-fangled inventions were expensive to build. They were tricky to drive, too, and difficult to repair when they broke down—which was often. A buyer not only had to have enough money to pay for a car built to order, but usually had to hire a chauffeur and a mechanic as well. Farmers and factory workers could not afford the contraptions, and most were not even sure they wanted one. "A horse always starts up," they said, "and it always gets there."

But the rich had great fun with the new toy. Society ladies decked out their cars with flowers and paper butterflies and drove them in automobile parades. They bought filmy veils to cover their hats and wore long coats called "dusters" to protect their dresses. Gentlemen sported goggles, driving gloves, and dusters, too. After all, motoring was a dusty business.

Some Detroit businessmen took an interest in Henry and his gas buggy. "It's the coming thing," they said. "There is sure to be money in it." So

they formed the Detroit Automobile Company and put up money to help Henry with the workers and materials he would need to manufacture gas buggies. As stockholders in the company, they would receive a share of the profits they expected Henry to make.

It was a good thing for Henry that these businessmen decided to support him. The Detroit Illuminating Company was becoming disgusted with him. "You work for the *electric* company," his boss said. "You could at least spend all your time on an *electric* car." At last they gave Henry a choice: his car or his job.

"I'll take my car," Henry said.

Now Henry had all the time in the world to perfect his gas buggy—and he took it. His backers stopped by to see him every few weeks. "Can't you hurry it up?" they asked. "The Oldsmobile Company is selling its pretty little touring car by the hundreds. We'll never make any money at this rate."

The truth was that Henry had not given them even one car to sell. Henry knew just what he wanted, and it was not a pretty little touring car. Henry wanted to make a car that was rugged, a car that could take the bumps and ruts of country roads, a car that a *farmer* would drive. "It's not quite ready," was the reply he gave whenever his backers came around.

Finally the backers stopped coming at all. They withdrew their money, and the Detroit Automobile Company was dissolved. Now Henry had no job and little money. He didn't seem to mind, though. He and a crackerjack mechanic known as Spider Huff were at work on a new project—a racing car.

As more and more people bought cars, racing quickly replaced parading as the popular automobile sport. Cars were no longer judged on style alone; now everyone thought that the best car was the fastest car. In the mid 1890s, just about the time Henry had built his gas buggy, the first official American track race had been held. But the cars had crawled along so slowly that the disappointed spectators had called out insulting remarks. So now mechanics were building cars especially for racing, and every race car driver was trying to be the first man ever to drive a mile in a minute.

When Henry's former backers heard that he was building a race car, they laughed. Why, he's never even sold a *passenger* car, they thought.

What in the world is he doing wasting his time building a race car? Henry knew very well what he was doing. If he could conquer speed and apply what he learned to his passenger car, he would have the finest car on the market, he reasoned.

Henry and Spider Huff finished their racer just in time to enter the "Great Race" to be held at Detroit's Grosse Pointe track. Henry signed them up for the ten-mile sweepstakes. The prize was to be $1,000. Henry needed that thousand dollars to continue work on his passenger car. He wanted to beat Henri Fournier, too. Fournier was the French racer who had come closest to the mile-a-minute goal. "I'm going to beat Fournier *and* Winton," Henry told Clara.

"Daredevil" Alexander Winton was the American track champion. That meant he was the leading car maker in America as well. Winton's manager was so sure that he would win the "Great Race" that he had picked out a huge cut-glass punch bowl set for the winner. It would look stunning in the Winton's big bay window, he thought.

Seven thousand spectators gathered at Grosse Pointe for the race. Everybody who was anybody

around Detroit was there, dressed to the hilt for the big event. A load of Winton's fans had come from Cleveland to cheer their hero on to yet another victory. Over 100 cars paraded out onto the track. But when the entrants saw how "Daredevil" Winton drove, they dropped out one by one. By the last race, there was nobody left to challenge Winton, nobody, that is, but Henry Ford.

Henry climbed up onto the toadstool-like seat of his little racer. Spider Huff clung to the runningboard—and they were off. The curves on those early tracks were steeply banked. Winton took them like the pro that he was. Henry had never driven in a race before in his life. Every time he came to a curve, he cut off the gas and swung wide. "Hang out!" he yelled to Huff. Spider hung out daringly to the side to keep them from turning over. Every time they came to the straightaways, Henry's trim little racer shot ahead. By the sixth lap, he and Winton were running side by side.

Suddenly Henry found himself driving through a cloud of black smoke. Winton's racer was having engine trouble. His mechanic dredged the bearings with oil, but it did no good. Henry shot ahead!

The crowd went wild. The very proper ladies of Detroit jumped up onto their seats. The very proper gentlemen threw their expensive hats into the air. One man whacked his hysterical wife on the head to settle her down. Henry swept to the finish.

Now Henry Ford was the American track champion. He hadn't broken the record for the mile, but he had come close to it. Newspapers splashed his name on their sports pages. Clara put the huge cut-glass punch bowl set on the hall landing of their tiny house. The $1,000 never came about. No one ever said just what became of it, but Henry was happy nevertheless. He had won his first race, and he had learned a lot about what makes a car cling to the road. He went back to his shop and applied what he had learned to his passenger car.

Chapter Four

Henry's old backers came running. "If a Ford can beat a Winton," they said, "it must be good." They formed a second company, the Henry Ford Automobile Company. "We're sure to make money this time," they told themselves. Still, they kept a close eye on Henry.

"And how is our car coming?" they asked at every visit.

"It's not quite ready yet," Henry always said.

The backers were not pleased. They called in a mechanic to inspect Henry's car. "It's fine—ready to go," the mechanic pronounced.

But there was just no hurrying Henry. "No car is going out for sale with my name on it until *I* say it's ready," he said.

His backers left Henry once again. The second Ford company was dissolved, just like the first. Henry was left with just $900—and the drawings for a new racer. He was convinced that building race cars was the way to improve the automobile. A car that could stand up to the rigors of racing could take anything. Henry was sure of it. Money or no money, Henry was not about to quit. He just did not believe in giving up.

Then along came Tom Cooper. Cooper was a famous bicycle racer. "I'll make you a deal," he told Henry. "I'll put up the money for your new racer if you will build me one just like it."

"You have yourself a deal," Henry said. He went to work on the 999 and the Arrow, a pair of racers named after record-breaking New York Central railroad trains. The "twins" were each 9 feet long, and they each had the power of 80 horses. (Most cars then had 10 to 12 horsepower.) "Why, the roar of the engines alone is enough to half kill a man," Henry said proudly.

At last the racers were ready to be tested. Henry didn't dare drive them through the streets of Detroit. He was afraid the roaring monsters would scare the citizens half out of their wits. Late one night, he went to the diner to talk to Night Owl John. Night Owl got out his horses and towed the two cars out to Grosse Pointe. Sleeping Detroit never heard a sound.

Henry tried out the cars. Tom Cooper tried out the cars. "What do you think?" Henry asked.

Cooper shook his head. "Frankly, they scare me to death," he said.

"I'd sooner go over Niagara Falls in a barrel myself than drive one of them in a race," Henry admitted.

Now there was a predicament. What good was a pair of racing monsters without anyone to drive them?

Then Tom Cooper thought of Barney Oldfield. Oldfield was a bicycle racer, too. "He'll try anything once," Cooper said.

So they brought Barney to Detroit. There was still one problem, though—Oldfield had never driven a car before. "You'll have a whole week to learn," Henry told him. Henry had signed up for another race at Grosse Pointe.

Oldfield took a look at the 999. "She's no bicycle," he said.

"All you have to do is keep the steering tiller straight," Henry explained. "That way, you can tell if you're still on the track."

Oldfield looked doubtful.

"I'll fix 'er up with *double* tillers," Henry said. "It will be just like steering your bike."

The following week Oldfield lined up with the other racers at Grosse Pointe for the Manufacturer's Challenge Cup. One of those other drivers was "Daredevil" Winton. Winton was determined to get his record back. He had built himself a brand-new racer just to be sure.

Oldfield stared straight ahead and let out the 999 at full speed. He didn't even cut off the power on the curves; he just pressed on like a madman. On the third lap, Winton's shiny new Bullet developed mechanical failure. Winton was forced to drop out of the race. A roaring monster pushed to the finish, its funny double tillers askew. It was the 999, of course, and in just 5 minutes and 28 seconds, a new American record. "Hurray for Oldfield!" the crowd cheered. "Hurray for Ford!"

The 999 had done just what Henry had wanted it to do—brought attention to the Ford name. It had taught him a lot about powerful engines, too. He went back to his shop and applied it all to his passenger car.

Chapter Five

Soon after the Manufacturer's Challenge Cup, a wealthy coal dealer came to see Henry. "I'm ready to stake my business on you," he said. Several other backers joined him. None of them had very much money, but they had great faith in Henry. They formed the third Ford automobile company—the Ford Motor Company—on June 13, 1903. On the sixteenth, the Ford Motor Company started business, and it is in business yet today.

Finally Henry had a car ready for sale—the Model A. By the end of the year, the new company had sold 650 Model As. But money for parts and labor seemed to go out as fast as car orders came in. The new backers were happy, though. Henry was selling cars! "Make us some more models," they said. "That's the way to sell cars. Keep 'em wanting a new model every year."

Henry did not agree. "A car should be like a fine watch," he said. "It should be built to last. Make one model and make it good. That's what I say."

His backers insisted on more models, though, so Henry built the Model C. "Build us a *fancy* car, an *expensive* car," his backers demanded. So Henry fancied up his Model B and presented it to them. It was a large touring car that sold for $2,000. The stockholders were pleased. Two thousand dollars per car sounded good to them.

Just when business was picking up, the Ford Motor Company began to get some bad news in the mail. Model A buyers all over the country had a complaint. It was true that the A could go 30 miles an hour, but it could *not* climb hills. Henry sent a mechanic out to each and every Model A owner, but it was too late. Confidence in the Ford name had already gone down. The company sold fewer and fewer cars.

"I've got to do something *spectacular*," Henry told Clara. He knew he had to do something to boost confidence in Ford cars. It was January. Detroit was freezing cold and buried under snow.

"I've got it!" Henry exclaimed. "I'll race the Arrow—on Lake St. Claire."

Clara was shocked. "*You* are going to drive the Arrow? On ice? Henry! Why not Tom Cooper? Why not Barney Oldfield?"

"I've got to do this myself," Henry insisted. "Just me and the Arrow in a race against time."

He told his backers to advertise the race. "And make certain you let it be known that the engine in our Model B is every bit as powerful as the Arrow's," he said.

A shivering crowd stood to watch Henry in this most unusual race. Everyone knew that race car drivers were daring. But race on ice? It was unheard of. A person would be crazy to attempt such a feat.

Henry walked out onto the frozen lake. The ice was full of cracks that were sure to be hazardous for a speeding car.

Henry, the non-quitter, was not about to back out. He vaulted into the Arrow and let her out at full speed. The crowd gasped. Clara hid her eyes. Ten-year-old Edsel looked on in dismay. At every crack, the Arrow took a giant leap into the air. "Just you keep coming down right side up," Henry muttered.

Finally it was over. Clara breathed a sigh of relief. The official timers came running. They flashed astounding news across the wires. Henry Ford had run his race against time in just 39 and 2/5 seconds, 7 seconds under the French record. Henry had just broken the world's record for the mile! And he had done it on ice.

The *Detroit Tribune* called Henry's ride the wildest in automobile history. The American Automobile Association demanded to see for themselves the official time sheets signed by the six timers and two surveyors. Yes, it was so. They placed Henry's record in a special "made on ice" category.

Henry began getting invitations to race from all over the country. In 1905 he received an invitation from Cape May, New Jersey. Victorian Cape May was America's most elite seaside resort. At low tide, its wide, beautifully smooth beach made an excellent race course. The gentlemen of Cape May had recently formed the Cape May Automobile Club.

"Ford is sure to set even greater records on our fine beach," they boasted.

A beach race. What fun! Henry had been building himself a new racer. He named it Beach Skimmer and headed east to Cape May. There was no way to drive a race car cross-country, so Henry shipped the Skimmer by rail and went by touring car himself. The Cape May races were set for a Friday and Saturday in August. By Thursday, quiet Cape May was full of honking cars. The Stockton Hotel was jammed with race car drivers and their supporters. A large crowd lined the sparkling white beach on Friday morning and spilled over into trolley cars set up for the comfort of the ladies. The races for touring cars driven by their owners came first.

What the crowd really wanted, though, was to see the giant racing machines driven by the pros. At last they appeared. On came Walter Christie in his big Blue Flyer. On came Willie Campbell in his big Red Flyer. On came Louis Chevrolet—without any car. On came Henry Ford—without any car. Something was obviously wrong.

The president of the Cape May Automobile Club stood up. "Ladies and gentlemen," he said. "We are most sorry to announce that the trials for racing machines must be delayed. It seems Mr. Chevrolet's Fiat, just arrived from France, is delayed in customs. Mr. Ford's car is still on a side track in Buffalo, New York." The disappointed crowd headed back to hotels and cottages.

It was just as well. In mid-afternoon a fierce northeastern storm set in. It lasted all night. The storm-tossed ocean cut up the beach. Men worked from dawn until race time trying to smooth out the ruts and gullies. A strong wind still whipped across the beach. The officials decided to reverse the course so that the wind would be at the drivers' backs. Racing today would be dangerous.

An eager crowd came despite a lingering drizzle. Everyone looked anxiously for Ford and Chevrolet, with cars this time they hoped. There they were! The Beach Skimmer and the Fiat had been delivered just in time.

But the races were disappointing. A giant wave hit Campbell's Flyer, nearly causing it to turn over. None of the drivers seemed able to come up to their usual daring speeds. Ford and Chevrolet protested to the judges. "We have not even had time to tune our cars," they said. The officials held a conference. Then they persuaded all the drivers to stay an extra night at the Stockton Hotel and race again in the morning. The disappointed crowd went home again.

A Cape May carpenter approached Henry. "You're welcome to tune 'er in my shop," he offered. In the midst of the delicate wooden stars and curlicues that decorated Cape May's houses, Henry greased and oiled his race car.

On Sunday morning, the racing machines were lined up once again. Henry drew the place closest to the ocean. And they were off. Henry was doing well until a giant wave spewed over the front of the Beach Skimmer. The Skimmer didn't stop, but the wash of water slowed her down, and Walter Christie shot to the finish.

Henry had lost. He did not even have the money to pay his bill at the Stockton, let alone the money to get home to Detroit. The year 1905 had not been a prosperous one. Along came Mr. Dan Focer, a Cape May railroad engineer who loved machines as much as Henry did. "It would make me most happy to pay your hotel bill and arrange for you and the Beach Skimmer to get back to Detroit," he told Henry.

Henry went home by train, leaving his touring car with Mr. Focer as assurance that he would repay his debt. The kindness was not forgotten. Henry never did come back to claim the car, and he made Dan Focer one of the first Ford dealers on the East Coast. The touring car put up for collateral sat in Focer Ford's show window for many years.

Around this same time, Henry went to a race in Palm Beach, Florida. He arrived to find that a large French race car had been wrecked on the beach. Henry walked around the heap that had only shortly before been a beautiful machine. He stooped down and picked up a shiny strip of metal from the ruined racer's body. It was unusually light, yet it had not been damaged. Henry handed it around to his mechanics. "What is it?" he asked. None of them knew. "Find out," Henry said.

The strip of metal turned out to be a type of steel with vanadium in it, made only in France. Henry hunted all over for an American steelmaker who could get his furnaces hot enough to make the unusual steel. Having found one at last, he went back to his factory and tore apart the new passenger car he was working on. He studied his car for all the ways he could use the new strong, but light, metal. Then he streamlined the model. It was 1908 before he finished.

The result was Henry's dream car—the Model T. Henry had put his heart and soul into the T; it was everything he thought a car should be. It was sturdy. It was reliable. It was large enough to hold an entire family. It was made of the finest materials, by the finest workers Henry could find. When he had a sample ready, he called in his backers. "From now on, I would like the Ford Motor Company to make this model and this model only," he announced.

The men looked at the plain little black box of a car. They looked at one another. At last one of them spoke. "It's so UGLY."

"Why must it be *black*?" one of the other disappointed onlookers asked.

"Anyone who wants a T a color other than black can just paint it himself," Henry said. "And another thing—our workers waste too much time scurrying around for tools and parts. From now on, the parts at Ford will be delivered to the workers."

Henry had worked out a moving chain that dropped off a specific car part to each worker.

The outcome was the beginning of assembly line manufacturing in America. In 1911 the Ford Motor Company moved to Highland Park. This new, modern factory was the largest automobile factory in the world. Henry Ford had become "Mr. Automobile." His company was soon turning out a Model T every 24 seconds. His superior engine, developed through racing, had become the cornerstone of the business. Ford Motor Company was now producing over 10,000 cars a year. By 1914 the number had jumped to a quarter of a million.

The Model T sold for just $600. For the first time in America, the average worker could afford a car. The T wasn't pretty, but it was rugged. It could take bumpy dirt roads as well as Henry's first little racer. It had a lightweight engine—as powerful as the 999's. It could hold its own on ice and snow like the Arrow, and, like the Beach Skimmer, no puddle was about to stop it. As if all this were not enough, the T was easy to repair. Inside every T was a little black book: *How to Repair Your Model T.* "Any farm boy could do it after milking," Henry said proudly.

Americans fell in love with the T. They wrote songs about it and sent Henry stories about it.

They gave it a nickname. It wasn't long before everybody had to have a "Tin Lizzie." Tin Lizzies poured out of Ford Motor Company factories in a steady stream all the way until 1926.

Farmers found the T just the thing for a quick dash into town when machinery broke down. They used it for hauling sick calves off to the veterinarian. They strapped goats to its running boards. One farmer even bundled a pair of pigs into the back seat and drove them oinking off to market. The farmers' wives saved their egg money all week, then drove merrily off to the mercantile for a well-earned Saturday of shopping.

Mailmen covered their routes in a third of the time. Firemen filled the T to the brim with hoses and buckets and raced off to put out fires.

But nobody took more pleasure in the Model T than Henry Ford himself. Henry had always loved picnics. Now, at the end of a hard week at the factory, his greatest joy was to ring up Clara and tell her to get a picnic basket ready. Clara would settle herself and the well-filled basket into the passenger seat. Henry would vault happily into the driver's seat, and off they would go for a day that would make any farm boy forget all about cows and milk stools.